·THE DONKEY'S TALE·

Mary Martin and Valerie Stumbles

Illustrated by Jean White

CASSELL

Cassell Educational Limited
Artillery House, Artillery Row, London SW1P 1RT

First published 1988

British Library Cataloguing in Publication Data
Martin, Mary
    The donkey's tale.
    1. Jesus Christ. Nativity — Dramatisations
    — For schools
    I. Title   II.   Stumbles, Valerie
    232.9′21

ISBN: 0 304 31571 0

Phototypesetting by Activity Ltd, Salisbury, Wiltshire
and MSS Studios, Dolgellau, Gwynedd, Wales
Printed and bound by the Hollen Street Press, Slough, Berkshire

Illustrated by Jean White

**A cassette of the music and songs
in this book is also available from
Cassell (ISBN 0 304 31578 8).**

Preface

The Donkey's Tale is the result of many hours of heart-searching, wondering how to produce a 'new' version of the Nativity. The Nativity has been presented in practically every way possible, so to come up with something totally original is virtually impossible. We gladly settled for something plausible! Our story is simple. Take the animals concerned with the Christmas story, add a piece of embroidery and there in one simple format is the Christmas story with a difference.

The songs are written to be accompanied by guitar and/or piano. The guitar chords are written to accompany the piano but for ease of fingering, capo options are written above. A few percussion suggestions are included.

We should like to dedicate this book to Mrs Pamela Ricketts and to the staff and children of West Rise Infant School, Eastbourne.

Mary Martin and Valerie Stumbles
West Rise Infant School, Eastbourne
Christmas 1987

The Donkey's Song

I worked for Jo-seph ma-ny years be-fore he took a wife. But now he asks the most of me, the jour-ney of my life. I must plod the road to Beth-le-hem, we have to tra-vel far. I'll car-ry Ma-ry all the way for she's going to have a child.

Everyone in Nazareth seemed to be busy. They were packing bags and loading their animals ready to return to their birthplaces where they were to be counted and taxed. Joseph, the local carpenter, was busy putting the finishing touches to a piece of furniture for a customer so he called to a couple of children nearby: 'Simon, Ruth, would you go and fetch my donkey from the field where he is grazing? I shall need him soon and I haven't got time to stop.' Simon and Ruth were only too glad to go and fetch the donkey for Joseph. They soon returned with Zebedee.

The Journey

Ambling along the dusty road___ carrying a heavy load.___ They rely on me.

They rely on me. I must not falter. Hurry _____ to Bethlehem, we've

got to be taxed today. Ambling along the dusty road___ I must be on my way.

Percussion suggestion : coconut shells throughout

Zebedee found himself being prepared for the long journey to Bethlehem. Soon he was off – it would be an adventure. On his back was Mary, Joseph's wife, who was expecting a baby. Night was falling, it was getting dark, but Zebedee was being led by his kind master Joseph.

Bethlehem

Percussion suggestion : side drum

The road to Bethlehem was very crowded. Zebedee moved slowly and carefully because he did not want to upset Mary. He found himself being passed by many other animals hurrying with their owners to various towns; they were anxious to get places to sleep for the night.

It was a long journey and soldiers everywhere hurried travellers to their destinations.

The Ox's Song

10

When Zebedee reached Bethlehem with Mary and Joseph there was very little room to spare anywhere. They searched and they searched and when they were about to give up, a friendly innkeeper said that they could stay in his stable. In the stable was a kind ox who didn't hesitate to move to one side and let Zebedee and his friends share the stall.

The Cockerel

v. 2 The cockerel crowed at break of day,
    Break of day, break of day,
    The cockerel crowed at break of day
    To welcome the new-born King.

Not long after they had settled into the stable, Zebedee watched a wonderful thing happen. Mary gave birth to a son. The baby was gently wrapped in swaddling clothes and laid in a manger. The Christ child gave a cry, disturbing a cockerel roosting close by and Zebedee heard him announce the birth.

The Lambs' Song

Teachers might find that this song is more comfortable played in E♭. To do this ignore the written key signature and use three flats instead, playing the music as written. In this case the capo should be up 1 on the guitar.

Percussion suggestion : maracas throughout.

Away in the distance, there were sheep grazing in the fields watched over by several shepherds. As the shepherds kept their watch, the heavens were filled with the sound of voices singing as angels appeared and one came down to tell the shepherds of the birth of the Christ child. The shepherds hurriedly prepared to travel to Bethlehem in search of the new-born King.

I'm a Camel

v. 2 I'm a camel, can't you see
      I'm as proud as proud can be.
      I'm following a brand-new star.
      It will lead me who knows where
      As I carry gifts so rare
      In search of a new-born King.

Percussion suggestion : sleigh bells

Even further away to the East, wise men had seen a special star appear. It lit up the night sky. They knew that it must be of great importance and so they loaded up their camels and followed the star.

The Mouse's Song

v. 2 In this stable so cosy and warm
I've seen Mary's baby newly born.
I've seen Mary so weary and tired,
Then someone smiled.

v. 3 I've seen angels appear in the sky
And their singing has filled heaven on high.
I've seen Mary so weary and tired,
Then someone smiled.

Unbeknown to Zebedee these shepherds and wise men were all travelling towards Bethlehem and the stable in which he was resting. But suddenly the sky appeared light as a giant star lit the sky and angels filled the skies with their singing. Startled, Zebedee stirred, and as he did so he noticed a little mouse creep from his corner under the straw and go to peep at the new-born babe.

Mary's Song

It was indeed a very happy sight for Zebedee to watch. Mary cradling her baby and Joseph looking proudly on. A turtle-dove quietly cooed contentedly in the rafters as Mary sang to her child.

Shepherds' Song

(Capo up 3)

Guitar

We have no-thing for a king ex-cept our love. We have no-thing for a king, ac-cept our love. As we

kneel in prayer to our king so rare. We have no-thing for a king ex-cept our love.

The night was calm and still. Soon the sky was much brighter than it had appeared ever before and Zebedee heard the bleating of sheep as shepherds arrived to give homage to the new-born King.

Holy Child

Mary and Joseph thanked the shepherds for their gift of love. They had also brought a new-born lamb who gambolled around the stable hoping Zebedee would play with him. Zebedee, tired, was more interested in the baby Jesus who was sleeping peacefully while Joseph and Mary sang a lullaby.

The Kings

Percussion suggestion : sleigh bells throughout

Then the wise men from the East discovered where the special star had led them. They found the stable in Bethlehem. Zebedee had never seen men of such finery. They were clothed with silks and covered with jewels. They had come to see the new-born King lying in a manger. They gave him their gifts of gold, frankincense and myrrh.

Angels' Song

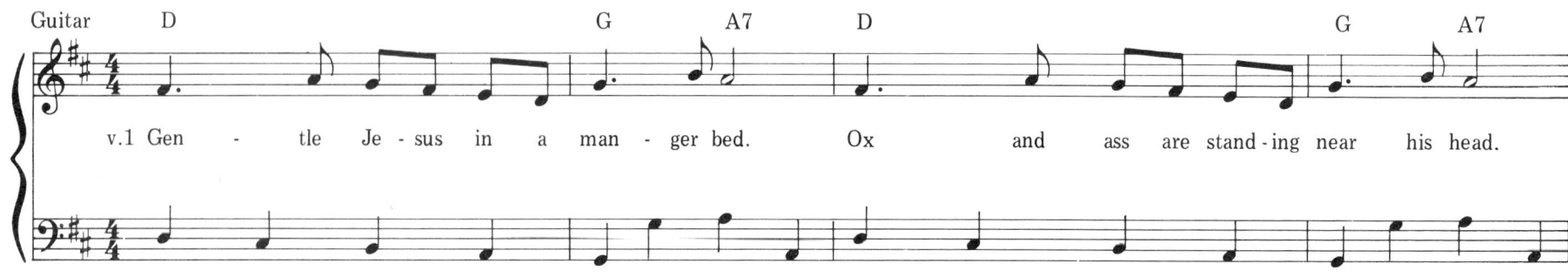

v.1 Gen - tle Je - sus in a man - ger bed. Ox and ass are stand - ing near his head.

An - gels in the sky —— sing to him a lul - la - by, —— sing to him a lul - la - by.

v. 2. Mary watches with a weary smile,
Born to her is this pure holy child.
Angels in the sky
Sing to him a lullaby,
Sing to him a lullaby.

28

Mary and Joseph were overwhelmed with all the love and gifts that were being showered on their baby. Zebedee noticed the tears welling up in Mary's eyes — she was so tired and yet so happy. She felt too tired to sing her lullaby but a chorus of angels arrived to sing for her. They sang to the visitors to the stable.

Hush, don't disturb Him

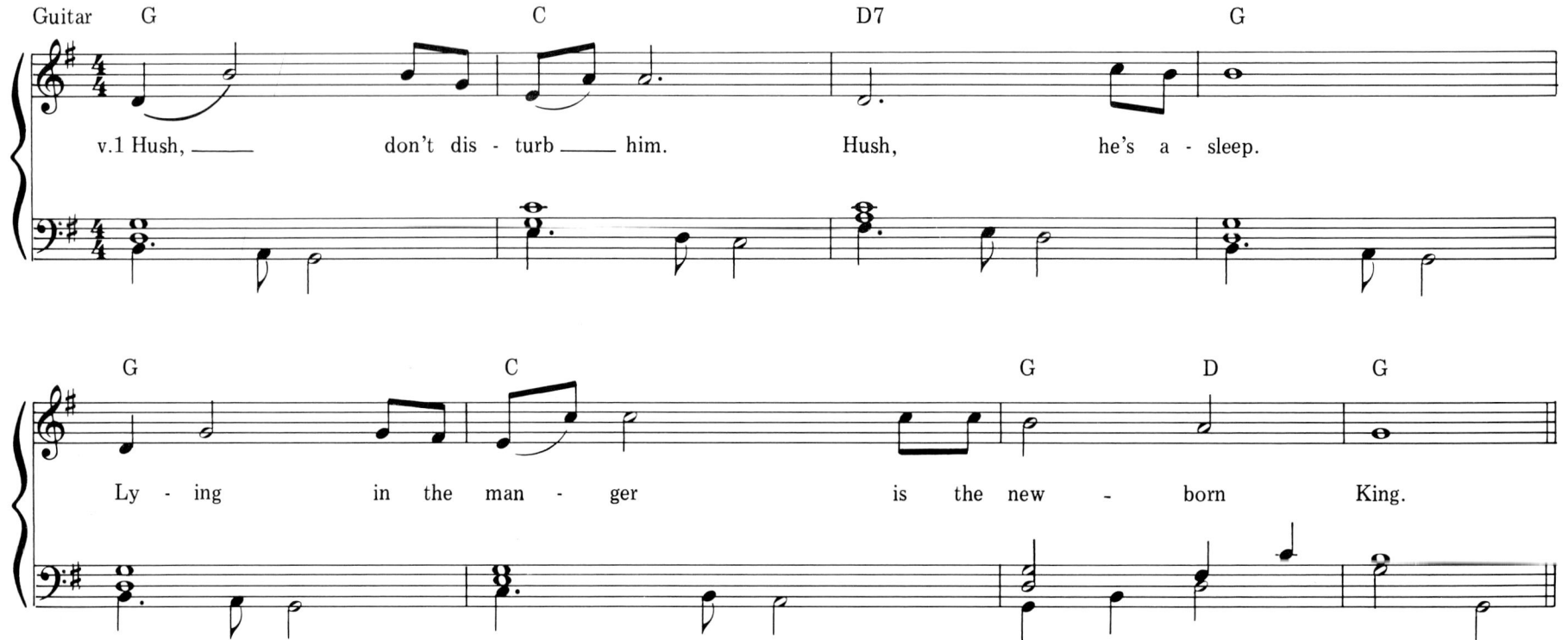

v. 2 Angels sing his praises.
Stars shine so bright.
Lying in the manger
Is the new-born King.

v. 3 Shepherds left the hillsides
For Bethlehem.
Lying in the manger
Is the new-born King.

v. 4 Wise men brought him treasures
From far away.
Lying in the manger
Is the new-born King.

v. 5 All here sing to Jesus,
Wondrous child.
Lying in the manger
Is the new-born King.

Percussion suggestion : chime bars

Zebedee felt humbled and very proud to be present at the birth of the Christ child. He had carried Mary many miles and over many rocky paths. His head began to nod and soon Zebedee was dreaming of the day's events, little knowing that his story and that of the ox, the rooster, the mouse, the dove and the lamb would be retold to this very day.